The Poetry Habit

The Poetry Habit

Kathryn Paulsen

Clare Songbirds
Publishing House

Clare Songbirds Publishing House Poetry Series
ISBN 978-1-957221-26-7
Clare Songbirds Publishing House
The Poetry Habit © 2025 Kathryn Paulsen

Printed in the United States of America
FIRST EDITION

140 Cottage Street
Auburn, New York 13021
www.claresongbirdspub.com

In memory of

Mrs. Smart:

Her married name,
but perfect for her
because
she was.

With a generation
of teens she shared
the joys of reading
literature

and of attempting
poetry.

Acknowledgments

"Radical Surgery" was first published in *Riddled With Arrows* and "A Used Paperback," in the *Books* anthology of Truth Serum Press. "Ghosts" is forthcoming on the substack site of the *Vincent Brothers Review*.

Thanks to Yaddo, Virginia Center for the Creative Arts, MacDowell, Ledig House (now Art Omi: Writers), and the Colrain Poetry Manuscript Conference.

Contents

Into the Deep Sea of Emily

. . .
Dive if you dare—
Don't forget to breathe—

Seize the Air

Please, no more love poems

I

Try writing about something else, he said.

So she did:

Death,
war,
sorcery,
deprivation
of sleep, lunacy, mathematics,
history
of imaginary
places and peoples,
geography
of remote
archipelagos (a word
she loved), the way the light
fell on feathers dropped .
from the wing of a bird
she can't identify,
the discipline
of watching a candle melt,
for hours, trying not to miss
the moment a single droplet of wax
glides down its side.

But these
didn't please
him either.

II

He wanted, he said,
to read what he'd never read before,
best
was when it didn't make recognizable
sense,
when he could imagine words tossed
in the air, caught,
made, taut and true,
into something new,
that he couldn't see through
or even into,
however long
and hard he tried.

At least he didn't say
write what you know or
lose the rhymes or
find
something else to make
with your
time.

Poetry

Poetry is a luxury
Available to [m]any
But also a necessity
That costs a pretty penny

Her Habit

She has
the poetry
habit bad

How come
it took her
so long

First Muse

"It was one of those fleshy summer affairs,"
the poet said, "You know the kind."
Not sure we do. The front row stared—
virginal, rabbity bookworms. He read a line.
It wasn't very fleshy. Hard to find
the girl under the words, but, oh, the words!
About-ness hardly mattered. She heard
a rush of wings, new music in her mind.
He looked a little wasted for his age—
what, twenty? He'd rushed in late,
sweaty, unkempt, as if just riz from bed,
but not from one of ours, dean forbid.
The next he read wasn't quite so great.
He yawned and stumbled on. She set pen to page.

A poem says . . .

Pay attention:
This word
Rhymes or not
This line
Stops or not
Runs over into
Another or not
For a reason

The reason is yours
To hunt down
Unscrabble
Reap
Keep

Not Always   but Sometimes

She gets lost
in a novel

and found
in a poem

Pinched

Poetry pinches your brain.
Nothing to be done for it,
but let the words spill out
and whip them into
[some kind of]
shape.

Trial by Verse

She wrote a letter; the letter would not right her
By hand of a better wordwright the ink wouldn't smear

The lines wouldn't draggle to the depths of the page
She'd never deny a second of her age

She only lied a little in not telling all
But that does not sufficiently justify acquittal

The eyes squeeze out at last their secret piques
Ink stains the fingers when the pen leaks

The One

Because this one's the right
one, the one and only
one, the one
she's meant for,
she can't bring
herself to write
even a slight
limerick or charm
for him for
fear of what might
turn out
wrong

A Poet . . .

Can write a poem
about anything. Really.
Whatever catches her eye
in the course of her day. That old
not-quite-lover she almost ran into
except that neither wanted
to be the first to acknowledge
having noticed the other.

Or she can harvest her dreams,
embroider her fantasies,
throw a few words at
the light that is always there
whether you notice it or not.

There is always some kind of
light—right? And there are plenty
of words for it. Some of them
will stick.

Radical Surgery

For the good of the poem

You must
cut
the confessional
the frivolous
the meaningless
the self-referential
the sentimental
the occasional
the accidental

You must
lose
the words that curdle
the lines that whine
the stanzas that abandon
the worst
of the night verse

You will
ache
to contemplate
what you've lost

You may
read it
alone
in times of need
if you must

Query

Wouldn't you like to see, read, consider, publish
some of her less-than-best?
It's pretty good, if she does
say so herself.
And there isn't enough
of her very best to go around

Words Lost and Found

Though sometimes these days
a word slips away

from view
for a second or two

her vocabulary has grown
larger with the years

so she's better
at crosswords and

at coming up with any
one of a goodly number of

livelier adjectives to
fix a dull spot or

verbs and nouns to
strengthen the bones

of an old poem or

a new letter.

Ghosts

All the writers
    I might have been,
        buried deep,
            haunt the sleep
                of the writer I am.

For Whatever Ails You

This doctor prescribes
a poem a day.
It will not be
just a placebo

but will engage your heart,
your mind, your imagination,
all of which need nourishment—

regardless of what the rest of you
is going through.

The Paste You've Been Waiting For!

To improve your teeth, breath, speech,
try your favorite phrases from the greatest
poems in the public domain—
Dickinson, Whitman, Wordsworth, Browning
Shakespeare, Sappho, Poe,
and others we could name—
printed in nutritious vegetable dye
on wholesome, digestible rice paper,
micronized and mixed into
a fluoride-free dentifricial base.
The FDA will doubtless disagree,
but we propose it may,
when used regularly,
also improve your memory.

Hatching

How much of the past
Can we keep alive
Before moving on?

How many letters
How often write
To how many friends?

There are limits
And there are those who fight,
Bite, rail, rage
Against the limits
And those who find
The limits multiplying
Like the dot in the center
Of box upon box
Upon box reflected
In mirror after mirror
After mirror—a person
A poem become
A vanishing point

For any moment

There's a poem
Often many
More than one

Poets in Hiding

Having been one herself,
she strongly suspects

they are many more than a minority
of everyone.

May they come out
and face their words.

Other Words

There's always another word
a different word
a word from another
language with more
syllables or fewer
a mouthful of a word
a word with only two
letters or even just
one

ready
for when
there's no word at all
and you are not
up to making
your own

The Word Might Be

disturbed
subdued
urgent
enough
tough
take
tick
The word might be digging, dipping, drowsy
The word might be dying
The word might be—
can only be—
what you make of it
You must make of it
what it needs to be,
honor the reason—
let it tell you—
why you brought it—
why it came—
out of your brain

I Planted These Words

I planted these words
years ago. Some are just now
beginning to grow.
If they die, I won't toss them.
They can at least be compost.

A Used Paperback

Her name—rich with vowels, and double
and repeated consonants, letters formed
round and regular—a perfect specimen
of penmanship—inscribed at the top
of the first page, above the author's
biography. Did she acquire it before
the stamp below: PAP ½ LIST?
Bought for a class in poetry, perhaps?

It doesn't seem the kind of work to appeal
to one with so careful a hand—but still—
did she read it—through and through and through—
did it thrill her—or did it leave her
just the same as before
it got to me—where did she go?

Numquam Satis

Sometimes it seems,
Reading literary magazines,
Which proliferate monthly, at the least,
In print, online,
That there is a surfeit of poetry:

So many words,
Refined, clichéd, crass, sublime,
Angry, soothing, polemical, anodyne,
Some hard to untangle, some way
Too nail-on-the-head,
Some you can't help stumbling over
As if the words were boulders,
Meant only to stop, to block.

But though you can
Sip but a drop
From that flood,

There can never be
Too much poetry.
There is never
Enough

I wrote a poem

Left it to grow
Lonely for so
Many years

Now it's here

Kathryn Paulsen's poetry and prose have appeared in publications from Canada to Ireland to Australia, including *New Letters, The New York Times, The Stinging Fly, Humber Literary Review, Scum, Craft, London Reader, Spillway.* and *Big Fiction.* She also writes novels, stage plays, and screenplays and earned an MFA in film at Columbia University. Kathryn has been awarded fellowships at Yaddo, MacDowell, and other retreats. She lives in New York City but, having grown up in an Air Force family, has roots in many places. See her occasional musings at ramblesandrevels.blogspot.com.